Our Leaders in Government

Heather E. Schwartz

Consultants

Regina Holland, Ed.S., *Henry County Schools*
Christina Noblet, Ed.S., *Paulding County
    School District*
Jennifer Troyer, *Paulding County Schools*

Publishing Credits

Rachelle Cracchiolo, M.S.Ed., *Publisher*
Conni Medina, M.A.Ed., *Managing Editor*
Emily R. Smith M.A.Ed., *Series Developer*
Diana Kenney, M.A.Ed., NBCT, *Content Director*
Torrey Maloof, *Editor*
Courtney Patterson, *Multimedia Designer*

Image Credits: pp.2, 17 (bottom), 31 LOC [HABS GA,61-
ATLA,7-]; pp.3,8 (bottom), 28 Associated Press; pp.3
(bottom), 21 LOC [LC-USZC4-599]; p.5 richard mittleman
/ Alamy Stock Photo; p.6 Phil Boorman/Getty Images; p.7
Jamie Grill/Getty Images; p.8 LOC [LC-USZ62-15349]; p.9
Tim Sloan/Getty Images; p.10 Jessica McGowan/Getty
Images; pp.12,32 Terry Ashe/Getty Images; pp.12-13
Jessica McGowan/Getty Images; p.13 Oli Scarff/Getty
Images; p.15 Frank Mullen/Getty Images; p.16 Paras
Griffin/Getty Images; p.17 (top) Associated Press; p.18
Michael Ledford/Getty Images; p.20 Bettmann/CORBIS;
p.23 Yuri Gripas/Getty Images; p.24 Klaas Lingbeek- van
Kranen/Getty Images; p.26 ZUMA Press, Inc. / Alamy
Stock Photo; All other images iStock and/or Shutterstock.

Library of Congress Cataloging-in-Publication Data

Names: Schwartz, Heather E., author.
Title: Our leaders in government / Heather E. Schwartz.
Description: Huntington Beach, CA : Teacher Created
Materials, 2016. |
    Includes index.
Identifiers: LCCN 2015042453 | ISBN 9781493825523
(pbk.)
Subjects: LCSH: Georgia--Politics and government--
Juvenile literature. |
    United States--Politics and government--Juvenile
literature.
Classification: LCC JK4316 .S35 2016 | DDC 320.4758/049-
-dc23
LC record available at http://lccn.loc.gov/2015042453

Teacher Created Materials

5301 Oceanus Drive
Huntington Beach, CA 92649-1030
http://www.tcmpub.com

ISBN 978-1-4938-2552-3

Table of Contents

24

21

Leading the Way

What if no one was in charge at your school? You could play all day and do silly things with your friends. It may sound like fun at first. But there would be problems, too! Students may fight or get hurt. Some students might not learn anything new.

Schools need leaders. Leaders help keep things in order and running smoothly.

CLASS RULES

1. Listen when others are talking.

2. Follow directions.

3. Keep hands, feet, and objects to yourself.

4. Work quietly and do not disturb others.

5. Show respect for school and personal property.

6. Work and play in a safe manner.

Your teacher is in charge of your classroom at school. He or she sets rules to help the class work and play together. Your teacher helps you learn. He or she is a leader.

There are other leaders at your school. Your principal is a leader, too. He or she makes sure the school stays safe and runs smoothly.

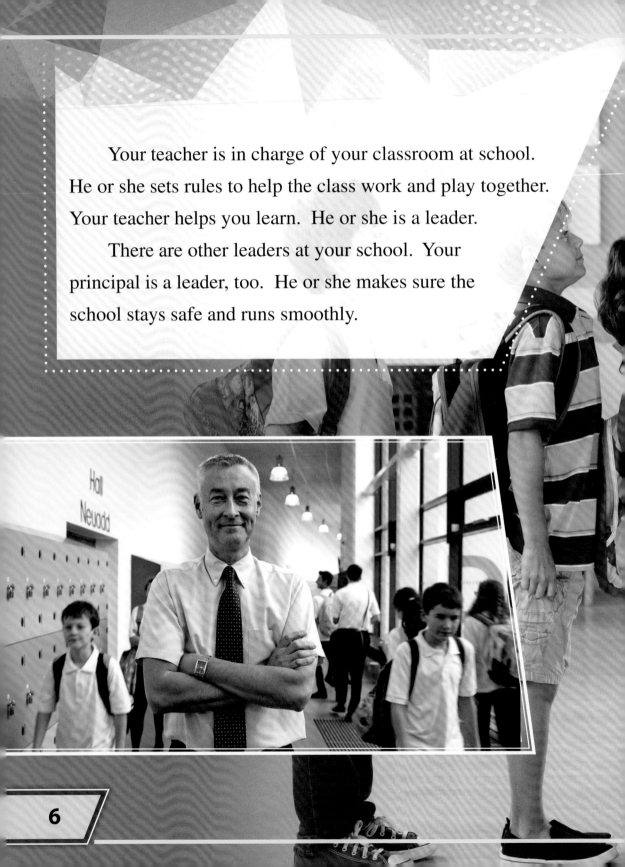

Wilson Lumpkin became **governor** of Georgia in 1831.

Washington, DC

Georgia

Kasim Reed became **mayor** of Atlanta in 2010.

Our **government** (GUHV-uhrn-muhnt) is made up of leaders, too. Each city and state has a government. So does our nation.

These government leaders have many tasks. They set rules. They make laws. They keep people safe. They help people live and work together.

George W. Bush became the 43rd U.S. president in 2001.

The United States is a **democracy** (dih-MAHK-ruh-see). That means we choose our leaders. We vote for them in **elections** (ih-LEK-shuhnz).

Voting for a leader is a big decision. People have to be smart when they vote. They have to learn about all the leaders. Then, they pick the one they think will do the best job.

Jason Carter, grandson of former president Jimmy Carter, runs for governor of Georgia in 2014.

Did You Know?

Long ago, the voting age was 21. In 1943, Georgia was the first state to let people vote at 18.

Voting
Today

oting A-K

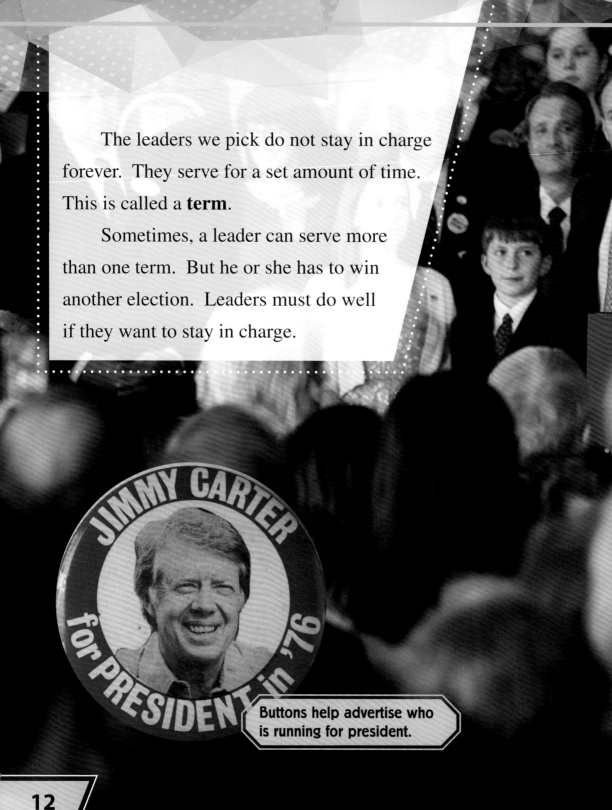

The leaders we pick do not stay in charge forever. They serve for a set amount of time. This is called a **term**.

Sometimes, a leader can serve more than one term. But he or she has to win another election. Leaders must do well if they want to stay in charge.

Buttons help advertise who is running for president.

Newt Gingrich tells people why he wants to be elected U.S. president.

Not by Choice

In some countries, leaders may take charge by force. Or they may be born into power.

Queen Elizabeth II of England inherited her power.

Meet the Mayor

A mayor is in charge of a city. He or she makes a **budget** (BUHD-juht). The budget tells how the city's money will be spent. The mayor is also part of the **city council**. It is a group of leaders who help the mayor. They all work together to help run the city.

Hartsfield-Jackson ✈ International Airport

A City First

Atlanta's first African American mayor was Maynard Jackson. Hartsfield-Jackson International Airport is named after him!

Maynard Jackson

A mayor lives in the city where he or she serves. The mayor's office is in City Hall.

You can take a tour of most city halls. You can tour Atlanta's City Hall. It was built in 1930. You may even catch a glimpse of the mayor on your tour!

Bill Campbell was mayor of Atlanta from 1994 through 2002.

Green Roof

Atlanta's city hall has a special roof covered in plants. It is called a *green roof*.

Greet the Governor

A governor is in charge of a state. In Georgia, the governor's term lasts four years. He or she helps create laws for the state. He or she works with a **cabinet**. It is a group of leaders. They help the governor run the state.

Governor Nathan Deal and baseball player Hank Aaron celebrate the construction of the Atlanta Braves stadium in 2014.

Georgia Governor's Mansion

Do you know where the governor of Georgia works? He or she works at the State Capitol building. It is in Atlanta.

The governor lives in Atlanta, too. He or she lives in a special house. It is called the Governor's Mansion (MAN-shuhn). It was built in 1967. It has 30 rooms. And there are three floors!

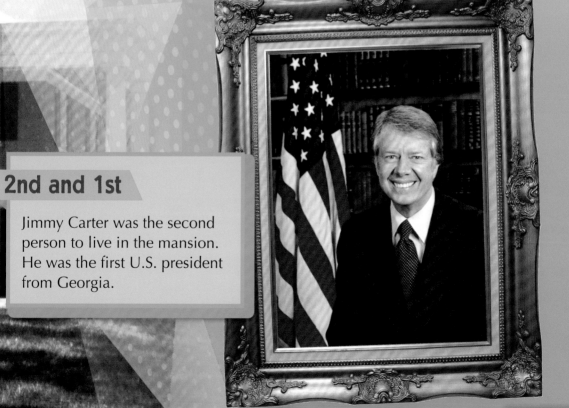

2nd and 1st

Jimmy Carter was the second person to live in the mansion. He was the first U.S. president from Georgia.

Power to the President

Do you know who is in charge of the whole country? Yes! It is the president! He or she leads the country. The president serves a four-year term. But he or she can be elected for two terms.

The president has many jobs. One is to approve the **federal** laws. These are the laws people must follow.

President Barack Obama

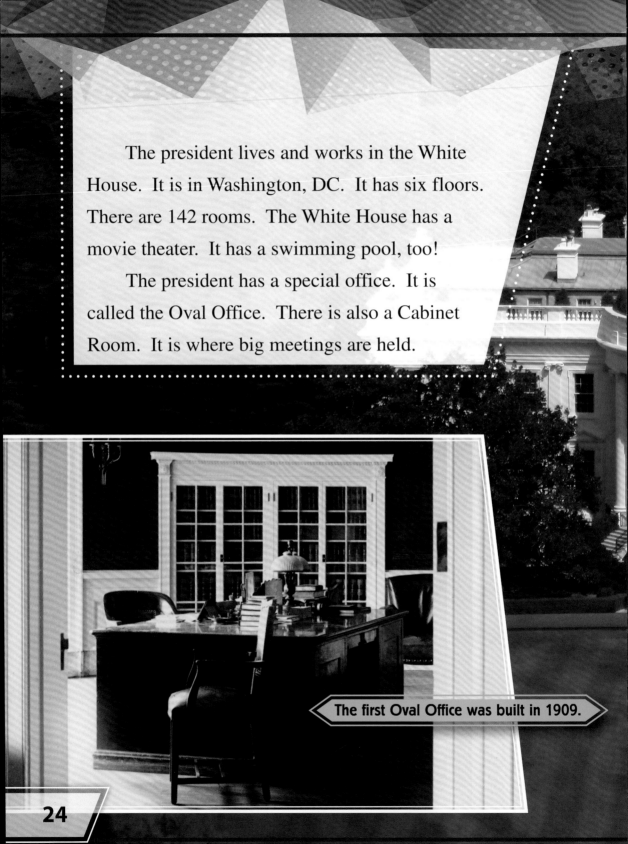

The president lives and works in the White House. It is in Washington, DC. It has six floors. There are 142 rooms. The White House has a movie theater. It has a swimming pool, too!

The president has a special office. It is called the Oval Office. There is also a Cabinet Room. It is where big meetings are held.

The first Oval Office was built in 1909.

Did You Know?

The White House is big! It takes 570 gallons of paint to cover the outside.

Be a Good Leader

We need good leaders in our country. Good leaders set fair rules and laws that help people work and live together.

You can be a good leader. Follow the rules. Obey the law. Help those in need. Be a good citizen. Make the country a better place!

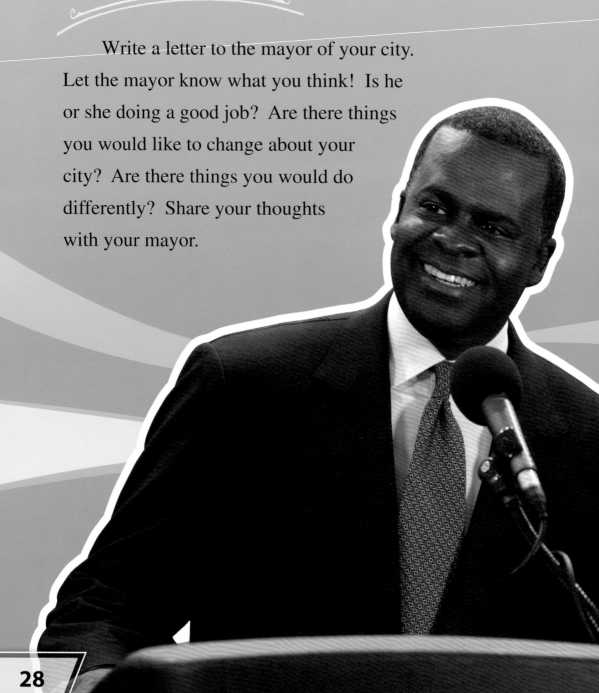

Share It!

Write a letter to the mayor of your city. Let the mayor know what you think! Is he or she doing a good job? Are there things you would like to change about your city? Are there things you would do differently? Share your thoughts with your mayor.

STATION NO. 19

CITY OF ATLANTA

19

Atlanta Fire

Glossary

budget—a plan for how to spend an amount of money

cabinet—a group of people who give advice to the leader of a government

city council—the group of people who make and change the laws of a city

democracy—a form of government in which people choose leaders by voting

elections—acts of voting for leaders

federal—relating to the government

government—a group of leaders who make choices for a country, state, or city

governor—the leader of a state or region

inherited—received money or property from someone who has died

mayor—the leader of a city or town

president—the leader of a country

term—length of time

Index

Running for President

When candidates run for president, they tell people what they believe. They talk about things they think are important. Pretend you are running for president of the United States. Write a speech to tell what is important to you. What promises will you make? How will you make sure to follow through on your promises?